Make Us ONE

A 31-DAY **Prayer Journey** TOWARD **Racial Healing**

COMPILED & EDITED BY
NIKO PEELE
AND **JONATHAN GRAF**

PRAYERSHOP
PUBLISHING

Terre Haute, Indiana

PrayerShop Publishing is the publishing arm of the Church Prayer Leaders Network. The Church Prayer Leaders Network exists to equip and inspire local churches and their prayer leaders in their desire to disciple their people in prayer and to become a "house of prayer for all nations." Its online store, prayershop.org, has more than 150 prayer resources available for purchase or download.

© 2020 PrayerShop Publishing

ISBN (Print): 978-1-970176-00-1
ISBN (E-Book): 978-1-970176-01-8

Since these prayers are based on the Scriptures, and pull language from the Scriptures but are not complete quotes, no single version of the Bible was used. In places where a complete verse might be quoted within the prayer, the appropriate version's abbreviation is placed following the quote.

1 2 3 4 5 | 2020 2021 2022 2023 2024

EDITORS' THANKS

We would like to thank all the individuals who submitted content—either a prayer or story—for this book. Not all the submitted prayers and stories were able to be used in the final version of *Make Us One*, but everyone's submission made this book what it is. Thank you.

We would also like to thank Dave Butts, chairman of America's National Prayer Committee (NPC), from whose members a majority of the prayers came, for his insight and vision for this project. We both serve as members of the NPC. We are forever grateful for the prophetic voice the NPC has, and for the direction Dave and the NPC's membership gave to this book.

Finally, we would like to thank our wives Carole Ann (Niko) and JoLyn (Jon) for putting up with us and praying for us as we worked on this project—especially evenings and weekends—during the months of July and August. Your gracious spirits toward us are deeply appreciated.

—Niko Peele and Jonathan Graf

CONTENTS

CONTENTS

CONTENTS

FOREWORD

"Confess your faults one to another, and pray one for another, that ye may be healed. The effectual fervent prayer of a righteous man availeth much." (Jas. 5:16, KJV)

Prayer plans and Bible reading plans are vital tools of spiritual weaponry in today's struggles. From this vantage point, I highly recommend *Make Us One*. This *31-Day Prayer Journey toward Racial Healing* is thought provoking and transformational.

This book is a must have read for your tool kit; an essential because seeking racial reconciliation in the 21st century is vital to the continuance of our growth and development as the human race. Therefore, in recommending this book, the most important message I can remind Humanity of is this:

We are created by God as "one blood":

> "And hath made of one blood all nations of men for to dwell on all the face of the earth, and hath determined the times before appointed, and the bounds of their habitation; That they should seek the Lord, if haply they might feel after him, and find him, though he be not far from every one of us: For in him we live, and move, and have our being; as certain also of your own poets have said, For we are also his offspring." (Acts 17:26-28, KJV)

God created all people of one blood. We are not separate races. We should not fight over skin color. We can see skin color. We're not colorblind. But we should "learn to live together as brothers," as my uncle Martin Luther King, Jr. said [and, I'll add, as sisters], "or perish together as fools."

During Martin Luther King Jr.'s lifetime, he said, "When we learn to value the human personality, we won't kill anybody."

I believe he would advise us to see each other as human beings, not separate races; not divided into selected races by socioeconomic differences, and certainly not by skin color. The concepts of separate races and racism are socially engineered, having no spiritual or scientific basis in fact.

This way of thinking comes from the socialization of humanity, not from God.

Social gospel is different from the Gospel of Jesus Christ. Social justice is weaker than God's justice, which is tempered by mercy, and redeemed by Christ's righteousness.

"Am I therefore become your enemy, because I tell you the truth?" (Gal. 4:16, KJV).

Martin Luther King Jr. was a preacher of the Gospel of Jesus Christ. So there again, he would remind us, "Listen to each other; communicate; love each other as brothers and sisters, not separate races."

This deliverance will require faith, hope, and love. Faith without works is dead. Faith works by love. That's in the Bible (Jas. 2:17; Gal. 5:6).

What is our work? Our work is to promote and share the love of God, in truth, to the born and to the unborn.

So faith is very important. We should have faith rather than fear. We should have love rather than hate. We should pray rather than panic.

As we do this and share the airways, and the written word, as we're doing today, I just pray that God will continue to hear us, guide us, and bring us together.

We are one blood, born and unborn, and God loves us. We have to learn to love each other.

Prayer:

Dear Heavenly Father, thank you for your everlasting goodness and love. I'm asking you right now to increase our faith, and love walk; to help us to "have [more] faith in God." Help us to "love [our] neighbor as [ourself]." Father, you desire for us to be healed and whole; "to prosper and be in good health even as [our] souls prosper." The socially engineered lie of separate races and racism blinds us. We repent of our clinging to skin color. Forgive us Lord. Open our eyes Lord. Jesus, you give sight to the blind. Show us your one blood/one human race. Show us, help us receive this truth together. Help us to love you, to love one another, and ourselves.

MAKE US ONE Lord. In Jesus' Name, by the power of your HOLY SPIRIT. Amen

Evangelist Alveda C. King
Founder of Alveda King Ministries
Co-Author of *We're not Colorblind*
Executive Director of Civil Rights for the Unborn

INTRODUCTION

You would have to be living in an absolute bubble away from any form of communication these days to not know that the subject of racism in the United States has come to the forefront and is causing hurt, anger, confusion and turmoil in the lives of many.

We believe the solution is Jesus, . . . and seeing in reality the answer to his prayer in John 17 to "make them (Christ-followers) one."

A Little Background

In the current day we are living in, it is painful to realize that systemic racism still bleeds into so much of our society.

Our nation's problem with ethnic prejudice and discrimination dates back to its inception. From the 1600s to the 1860s, our forefathers enslaved more than 10 million Africans, bringing them to work in American homes and on plantations.

Even though our new country's "Declaration of Independence" stated that "all men are created equal, that they are endowed by their Creator with certain unalienable Rights, that among these are Life, Liberty and the pursuit of Happiness," sadly, it did not work out that way for blacks and Native Americans. Slavery, along with the unjust treatment of Native Americans, is often referred to as "America's Original Sin."

Ultimately, a growing abolitionist movement, fueled with fervent prayer and collaborative efforts to eradicate slavery, eventually led our nation into one of its bloodiest battles, The Civil War. The outcome was a victory that ended slavery. The fight for full freedom, however, has continued even up to today as the opposition toward minorities and people of color remained steadfast. While certainly racist attitudes and actions have improved since 1865-1960s, there is still work that needs to be done and healing that needs to take place.

America's problem with race has not been limited to the historic black and white racial divide but also toward other ethnic groups such as Native Americans, Japanese, Hispanics, etc.

It's time Church!

While prejudice and discriminatory acts toward people because of their color, class, and culture are still a reality in our country, we have also seen justice rising over this issue. Much of the lasting progress made over the past decades has been accomplished through God-fearing believers.

As new social justice and civil rights movements are pushing to dominate the narrative, the Church carries the kind of justice that meets both the temporal and eternal freedom that the world is searching for. It is a Jesus-justice fueled by biblical conviction, compassion, prayer, and action that will bring revival to the heart and transformation to society.

In this critical moment in history we cannot overlook the urgency of the hour. It is time for the Church to rally and call our nation into what Dr. Martin Luther King called "a higher level of justice." There is only *ONE* true answer to healing the racial divide in our nation, and it is Jesus, seen through the public witness of the multi-ethnic Church. It is time to unify as the one Body we already are in Christ.

One of the most powerful prayers recorded in Scripture is when Jesus prayed for us, the Church, in John 17:21: "I pray that they will all be one, just as you and I are one . . . so that the world will believe you sent me" (NIV). Jesus was crying out for not only vertical reconciliation but also horizontal, a oneness that will draw the world into an intimate relationship with the Father and with each other.

It is a sad truth that the Church is still one of the most segregated spaces in our society. That is because the enemy knows the power of oneness. It is his greatest tactic to keep the Church divided. Why? Because it will be the most powerful witness when the multi-ethnic Church begins to operate as one Body, releasing righteousness and justice on the earth. This oneness with God and with one another screams to the world that we are all made in His image, and that knowing Jesus is the way to oneness with Him.

Why *Make Us One*?

This book is written to invite us—to invite you—into a "higher level of justice" through joining in with the ongoing intercession of Jesus: *Oh that we would be one, just as you, Jesus, and the Father are one, that the world would know the Father sent you! That oneness would be manifest in our families, communities, cities, states, and nations!*

True and lasting transformation can only be born and sustained from the posture of prayer. *The place of prayer is the utmost powerful and beautiful place on the Earth.*

This book is a compilation of prayers written by both seasoned and emerging voices in the Body of Christ. Many of these leaders have been on the frontlines of prayer, of action, and of racial reconciliation for decades. Their years of experience and plowing unleash great faith through their words. There are also personal stories from those who have experienced the pain of discrimination based on their ethnicity and color of their skin. These stories have been included in order to help us to perhaps see our own underlying implicit biases and empower us to replace them with the biblical truth: we are one race and one blood made in the image of God and everyone should be treated as such.

Why do I need this?

Some of you may be thinking, *I'm not prejudiced; I am not a racist. Why should I pray through this book?* Or if you are not white, you may be thinking, *This is for white people. They need this. I don't.*

Here are four quick reasons you should pray through this book:

1. If you desire what Jesus desired for his Church—that we be one—then you need to pray through this for his sake and the sake of his Church!

2. The power of a truly unified Church that stands against the sin of racism will have an immense influence on the healing of our nation. Be a part of that with your prayers.

3. Practice "identificational repentance." In Daniel 9, Daniel prays a powerful prayer asking God to forgive Israel of all the sins that had caused him to punish Israel and send them into exile in Babylon. Daniel had not committed those sins! Why did he need to ask forgiveness for them? Because God wanted him to identify with the sins of his ancestors, repent and confess them, so forgiveness and healing could flow. I (Jon, the white guy) believe that is the posture the white Church in America should take in this day—identify with the sins of our white ancestors and repent for them—so God's healing and blessing can flow.

4. You might be surprised at what happens. I have been an intercessor long enough to know that when we pray over an issue with sincerity, we get God's heart on the matter. We begin to see what he sees. When we pray, one of the first things that happens is that the Holy Spirit shines his light on our own heart. Pray through this and let that happen!

Start the Journey

Our prayer is that as you embark on this 31-day prayer journey you will be transformed inwardly in order to produce outward transformation in your daily life and within your sphere of influence. We believe that as you allow God to take you deeper and to search your own heart, you will be awakened with the awestruck wonder of His image in all of humanity. I also encourage you, don't take this journey alone. Take this prayer journey together with your family, friends, small groups, and church. Have everyone pray through a copy.

Most prayers and testimonies end with a section "What is the Holy Spirit saying to me?," which includes space to write down what the Holy Spirit is speaking to your heart. Don't skip over this activity. Pause at the end of each day or story and ask the Holy Spirit to speak to you. Listen. Write it down! Then share your experience of what the Holy Spirit is teaching you with each other.

We truly believe the Father wants to bring racial healing to the nation, through a unified Church. Be a part of that. Lord Jesus, make us one.

—Niko Peele and Jonathan Graf

Open My
Eyes

F ather, I pray that the eyes of my heart may be enlightened in order that I may know the hope to which you have called me, the riches of your glorious inheritance in your holy people. Father, your intent was that now, through the church, your manifold wisdom should be made known to the rulers and authorities in the heavenly realms, according to your eternal purpose that you accomplished in Christ Jesus our Lord.

Lord, open my eyes to see the many sides of your wisdom as it is manifested in the numerous ethnicities, cultures, and colors of your people. Help me to see that the greatest riches of this earth are found in people from various contexts, experiences and expressions. Remove any lens over my eyes that darkens the image of God manifested in those who look, think, act, and worship differently than me. Jesus, help me to see your image in everyone I meet.

In this hour Jesus, you have ordained the Church to be a light in darkness. Tune my ears to hear your wisdom. Cause me to feel your heart. I desire to experience the divine riches you have hidden in every nation, tribe, and tongue. I pray that you would help me to see people the way you see them so that I may love them the way you love them.

Jesus, as you were moved with compassion to weep with Mary and Martha, move me with compassion to mourn with those who mourn. Let me be quick to listen, slow to speak, and slow to be angry. Help me esteem others more highly than myself. Teach me to seek to understand before seeking to be understood. Give me eyes to see and ears to hear what the Spirit is saying to the Church and what people are saying to me.

Finally, Father I pray that you pour out your Spirit upon me that I may be bold and courageous. Help me to do justice, love mercy and walk humbly before you, God. Jesus, as you reconcile all things, I pray you use me to help reconcile the deepest divisions in my community and our nation. Let your Kingdom come, let your will be done. In Jesus' name. Amen.

Corey Lee is a husband, father of four, pastor, and movement leader among America's historically black colleges and universities. He seeks to see unity in the church across denominations, generations, and cultures.

(Eph. 1:18, 3:10-11; Jas. 1:19; Phil. 2:3; Micah 6:8)

WHAT IS THE **HOLY SPIRIT** SAYING TO ME?

I Decrease, That You Would Increase

Lord, humble us.

    Make us go low. Make us lay prostrate.

Make us weak so that your strength will prevail during these times.

Help us to see how small and feeble we truly are.

Help us to see that we can do nothing apart from your grace and power.

As we decrease, it is the cry of our heart that you will increase!

In this battle to end racism and racial inequality in our land, would you clothe us with humility?

In this fight to stand for righteousness and justice, help us not to lose our Christlikeness!

We pray that true Christlike humility will clothe everything we do and say in this hour.

Would you anoint your bride and servants to be clothed with both courage and humility?

Help us Lord. Help us Lord!

(John 3:30)

Will Chung, along with his wife **Andrea,** are the co-founders of The Meeting Place (TMP) based in Southern California. The TMP is a prayer and training center aiming to raise up spiritual leaders who make a kingdom impact where they are.

WHAT IS THE
HOLY SPIRIT
SAYING TO ME?

Search Me, Help Me, Teach Me

Father, when we think of all the hurtful things that have been done to others who are your image-bearers, we are broken-hearted. Even if we feel as though we have not personally offended, we number ourselves with the transgressors in identificational prayer because we are part of the Body of Christ. When one of us offends, all are guilty; when one of us is hurt, all of us hurt. Because we have believed in your Son's work on the cross, we are your children—brothers and sisters and joint-heirs with Christ, our brother.

Help us to learn to love with the kind of love that defines you—you are love. Even if we take up all kinds of causes, if we don't have love it isn't worth anything. Help us to be patient and kind as we seek to understand one another. Help us not to be jealous, boastful, proud, or rude. Show us when we're being demanding. Help us to learn from the past without keeping a record of being wronged, for you have said that you are our avenger and you will repay justly.

Teach us not to rejoice over injustice but to rejoice when truth

Sandra Higley is a mostly retired member of the editorial team at David C Cook Publishers. Her intercessory assignments include standing in the gap by "praying the hard stuff" and worshiping God over people during difficult situations.

wins out. Keep us from giving up or losing faith during these difficult times. Keep hope alive in us as we endure through difficult circumstances—for your glory, Father, and the glory of your dear Son.

(Gen. 1:26; Mark 15:28; 1 Cor. 12:13, 21, 26;
1 John 4:8; 1 Cor. 13:3-7; Rom. 12:19)

WHAT IS THE
HOLY SPIRIT
SAYING TO ME?

Move Me Closer

Father, Jesus said that nation would rise against nation, and kingdom against kingdom. But that would be just the beginning of the birth pains. The subject of race is one of the most discussed topics in our culture today. Racism is one of the most basic and deadly problems in history and it is increasing in power at this time.

However, we know the Church is called to be different. Father, you call us to "move closer" to you and to one another. This problem of racism only changes if we change, from up close. It's easy to judge what we don't understand, but everything changes when we move closer to one another.

▸ Father, forgive us for thinking that some races are better than others.

▸ Father, forgive us for thinking that there is something better in us than in others.

▸ Father, forgive us for showing favoritism when we are all undeserving of your mercy and grace.

▸ Father, forgive us for our pride, feeling sufficient in ourselves, that we don't need God or anyone else.

▸ Father, forgive us for judging based on externals.

▸ Father, forgive us for our insecurity, for being afraid of those who are different and those we can't control.

> Father, forgive us for not being a house of prayer for all nations, for every race.

> Father, forgive us for partnering with Satan, the accuser of the brethren rather than partnering with your Son, the Lord Jesus, who ever lives to intercede

Dr. Jason Hubbard is the executive coordinator of the International Prayer Council, which networks prayer leaders and prayer networks around the world.

> Father, forgive us for separating ourselves from one another

Father, help us learn to "listen" to one another.

Father, may we "move closer" to you and to one another.

In the Name of Jesus, Amen

(Matt. 24:7-8; Heb 7:25)

WHAT IS THE HOLY SPIRIT SAYING TO ME?

Momentary Hurt, Lasting Memories

I remember the first time I experienced racism as a child and was aware of it. I was about seven years old.

I was attending a summer camp in Michigan. It was a rather prestigious camp, and I was the only person of color there.

One afternoon, we were playing a game where all of the kids would tackle the counselor. This single event would forever open a young boy's eyes to his difference. I was singled out that day for the roughness with which I was playing. I was told that when I hit, my hands left a mark. But I was a rather mild-mannered child, and there were dozens of kids playing the game. There would have been practically no way to pick out the impact or impression of a single child's hand in this instance.

I was placed in a caged space alone as a punishment until my parents came to pick me up later that day. Needless to say, I never went back to that camp.

It was years later as a high school student that I remember first being called a "nigger." I attended a small, conservative, Christian school. Mostly white. Like most of my black counterparts, I always felt different, but never overtly discriminated against. That's the problem with subliminal racism. You can't see it or hear it. But it is felt.

There was, however, a pending curiosity that I often felt from my peers. As a high-achieving, communicable black young man, my peers were repeatedly shocked at the fact that my natural abili-

ties and my blackness could coexist together. It didn't fit the stereo-
types that they had seen on television or heard about around the
dinner table. In high school, a black student was like a new species
coming into the camp, especially for my many white counterparts
who had never had a black classmate or friend, and vice versa.

As we grew more familiar with one another, more of those
subdued perceptions and learned behaviors emerged. One day, in
the locker room during P.E., one of the upperclassmen took his full
liberty with me, when, in jest, he called me a nigger.

I will never forget the way that word made me feel the first
time it was used by a white man to address me. It totally disarmed
me; then it enraged me. Then it summoned me to address the po-
tency of the moment that it created with now dozens of onlookers
awaiting my response.

While he said it in jest, this flagrant display of testy ignorance
invoked something deep within me. In a single moment, the history
of my parents, grandparents, and ancestors who had all experienced racism—whether in the form of racial profiling, Jim Crow,
slavery, or the like—flooded my heart and mind, and with the
righteous indignation and authority that only those memories can
bring, I responded sternly with resolve and solemnity: "You will
never call me that again."

Although deeply upsetting in the moment, I still continued
to respect and admire the young man who used this foul word to
address me. He was a friend, and he continued to be.

One act of racism does not make a person inherently racist. It
does, however, uncover patterns of unaddressed bigotry, suprema-
cist thinking, and ignorance that need be addressed.

Spoken words have consequences. For instance, this careless
and flippant word inflicted a wound to my soul that would heal,
but its impression left a memory that is permanently etched in my

mind, and into the minds of the observers who have brought it up to me again, years after the incident occurred.

When we experience racism, it never happens in a vacuum. It is often felt on many levels. May God grant us all sensitivity to the implications of our shared history. And may we learn to honor, love, and forgive one another as we move toward a unified future of reconciliation and inclusive equity.

Dexter Sullivan is the founder of Dexter Sullivan Ministries (DSM), a 501(c)3 organization committed to reaching, loving, and building people and communities. DSM has partnered with 20 nations globally and the majority of the United States with an emphasis on prayer, transformation, and philanthropy.

WHAT IS THE HOLY SPIRIT SAYING TO ME?

▼

We proclaim that Jesus

is the light of the world.

Help us to see all people,

in all their array of

colors and diversity,

as manifestations of your light,

for we are all created

in your image and are

sacred in your sight.

▲

Jesus, Awaken Me with Light

Father, your word tells us that you are our light and salvation. I and my brothers and sisters acknowledge that now, more than ever, we need your light to shine in the darkness of the culture that threatens to overtake our nation, our churches, our neighborhoods, our homes, and our hearts. You are our only source of redemption and healing.

We proclaim that Jesus is the light of the world. Help us to see all people, in all their array of colors and diversity, as manifestations of your light, for we are all created in your image and are sacred in your sight. Shine your light in our hearts, dispelling any place of prejudice, for in your light we see light. With boldness and courage, we ask you to change us in any way you desire.

Empower us to love others in the same way you love each of us personally. Awaken our ears to hear the pain and suffering of others. May we also be quick to extend our hands in service, for we do not only love with words, but also with action.

We are in awe that you have commissioned us to live as light

Rebecca Shirey travels internationally as a Bible teacher/speaker, having delivered keynote sessions in 12 foreign countries and across the United States. She and her husband, Lou, serve on America's National Prayer Committee and are recognized prayer teachers in the International Pentecostal Holiness denomination.

bearers. As agents of your light and dispensers of your love, we speak grace and peace over fractured families, over our national discord, and racial unrest. May we live collectively as "the city on the hill" that gives light to everyone and brings glory to God.

We ask this in your name. Amen.

(Ps. 27:1; 36:9; Matt. 5:14-16)

WHAT IS THE
HOLY SPIRIT
SAYING TO ME?

Forgive Us, Restore Us

O ur loving heavenly Father, we come to you in the most powerful Name of Jesus. We worship and praise you with every breath that is within us. For it is truly in you alone that we live and move and have our very being.

We are desperately seeking you during this very chaotic time. Our nation is in a spiritually war-torn state. Please cleanse us, forgive us, revive us, transform us, heal us! We cry out to you to intervene and bring healing to our minds and hearts from any hatred, hurt, pain, confusion, or misunderstandings.

Search the depths of our souls and reveal anything contrary to your Word that hinders the process of healing that needs to take place in our nation. Help us to be real and honest with you, ourselves, and others. Remove any pride and blind spots that keep us from accepting each other and becoming united in the body of Christ and our country.

Forgive us for the sin of racism that is an age-old strategy and lie of the enemy which makes us feel or think that we are better, more important, more valuable or superior than someone who looks different from us in color, ethnicity, nationality, wealth, or culture.

Forgive America for the part it played in slavery and racism in our country's formation as this issue continues to plague us again.

Help us to be patient with one another and to listen and learn from one another's differences. Help us to show empathy with others even if we don't understand or agree with their point of view.

Pat Chen is a board member of the National Day of Prayer and America's National Prayer Committee. She is the president of First Love Ministries International, a prayer ministry located in the San Francisco Bay Area and Washington, DC.

Father, restore to us a holy reverence and fear of God and a fresh revelation and understanding of your Word in Genesis 1:26 and Acts 17:26, which declares that we are all created from one blood and are all made in your image after your likeness. Penetrate this truth so deeply within us that we are able to celebrate the fact that we are all part of the same human race, regardless of our skin color or background. Saturate us with your love that we may embrace our calling as reconcilers and healers.

We expect to see a great spiritual awakening because we know your eyes are on the righteous and your ears are attentive to our prayer. We realize it is not by our own might nor by our own power, but it is by your Holy Spirit that this battle will be won! For you are the Warrior, The Lord is your name. Thank you for being who you are and hearing our prayer. In Jesus' Name. Amen.

(Acts 17:28; Gen. 1:26; Acts 17:26; 1 Pet. 3:12; Zech. 4:6; Ex. 15:3)

WHAT IS THE **HOLY SPIRIT** SAYING TO ME?

_____

_____

_____

_____

_____

We Repent of Historical Sins

Triune God and creator of all, we come to you as desperate people. You know our thoughts before we think them and our words before we speak. Lord, cleanse us for not obeying your word to love one another as you love us. At creation, you said, "Let us make humanity in our image." When we mistreat any of the people you created, we attack your image and are guilty of sin. Forgive our sin of racism, silence, and denial. We see the result of our sin in our cities, our nation, the world and people everywhere.

Our racism, silence and denial have made it acceptable to injure, victimize, exploit, wound and kill your people. Our racism has been evident against many, especially black Americans, who have suffered the indignity of slavery, segregation and discrimination in America for hundreds of years. When Miriam and Aaron spoke against Moses for his marriage to an Ethiopian woman, you struck Miriam with leprosy. The body of Christ has leprosy!

The Church has been complicit over the hate, murder and displacement of Native Americans. We enacted racist and discriminatory policies with Chinese and other ethnic groups who immigrated to America. During World War 2, we interned Japanese Americans in camps which destroyed their lives and livelihoods. We need cleansing, Lord.

We have not only remained silent but we have also denied the reality of racism. Our denial has prolonged suffering and obstructed healing of wounds we caused. Some of us are privileged due to the color of our skin. Forgive us for either not knowing or denying this truth. Purify us from unrighteousness.

You abolished inequality when you died on the cross. There is neither Jew nor Greek, slave nor free, male or female in you; we are all one in Christ Jesus. Lord, as a Church, we admit our racism, silence and denial which has divided our country. Let us be a people who praise you and bless all those made in your image. We repent and seek your power to change direction.

Judy Turpen served as the chair of prayer ministries for Christian Educators Association International (CEAI), a non-profit association for public and private school educators for 30 plus years. She is the author of "Public Schools: Power Prayers," a booklet on praying for teachers and public schools.

I ask forgiveness for your Church, and as a part of that body, I ask forgiveness for myself. I say I love you who I have not seen and yet, have not loved my brothers and sisters whom I have seen. Search my heart and show me its wicked, racist ways. God, give me wisdom to unlearn beliefs and behaviors of the past. Help me speak up in the future when I hear words and see behaviors that do not align with your heart. Help me heal personally as our nation heals. May I love with my words and by my actions. In Jesus Name. Amen.

(John 15:12; Num. 12:1-10; Eph. 2:14; Gen. 1:26; Mk. 3:25; Jas. 2:9; I John 1:9, 4:20; Ps. 139:23, 24; I John 3:18)

WHAT IS THE HOLY SPIRIT SAYING TO ME?

One Race

ather, your Word tells us that every nation of men to dwell on all the face of the earth have all been made of one blood. Regardless of the color of our skin or where we live, we are all of one race—the human race. Forgive us—forgive me—for magnifying the flesh, for the flesh profits nothing.

Transform us to be like you, a people who look at the heart and see every person as you see them. Each one of us is made in your image.

This is astonishing and reason for great joy and wonder. Help us to value every human life as you do, and to put behind us our focus on the flesh—and the strife produced by it. Teach us to celebrate our similarities—the important matters of heart and mind and soul and spirit; of common human experiences, the wonder of being filled with your Spirit and the indescribable joy of experiencing and praising you!

Give us your eyes to see people as you see them and enable me, by the power of your Spirit, to love them as you love them . . . and as you love me. In Jesus' name, Amen.

(Acts 17:26; John 6:63;
1 Sam. 16:7; Gen. 1:26)

Cynthia Scott is involved in prayer ministry and local ministry initiatives in Pittsburgh, Pennsylvania. She also served as national prayer coordinator for Franklin Graham's Decision America Tour and continues to work with the Billy Graham Evangelistic Association.

WHAT IS THE **HOLY SPIRIT** SAYING TO ME?

Not My Daughter!

My story begins while I was in college. I was a working student at the time.

I was dating a white girl. We dated for seven months. But her parents never knew that I was her African American boyfriend. Whenever I would see them, they solely thought that I was a friend, not her boyfriend.

After some months of dating I asked her if her parents knew that I, a black man, was in a relationship with her. She paused and told me, "I can't lie to you. No, they don't know. They only see you as my friend. Nothing more."

I asked her why she hadn't been honest with them and told them I was her boyfriend, especially since we had been dating for so long.

She replied, "You don't know them like I do. If they were to find out that you were my boyfriend, they would disown me as their daughter. They are that crazy. They do not believe in interracial marriage, despite going to a multicultural church."

She said, "You know my dad is a cop. If he knew, that may make things worse for you."

I took this to heart and thought it over. I understood, but I did not like the situation. Christmas was soon coming and I wanted to give her a gift, but school was out. I dropped the gift in her mailbox, and told her to check the mail before her parents could.

I called her to make sure she had received it.

But her parents found the gift and began to question her about it and demanded to know who it was from. It was a more intimate gift than just a friend would have given. They were confused since they were under the assumption that we were just friends.

Joshua Timberlake is married to Kristen Timberlake, and they have a daughter, Zoë Celeste. Joshua and Kristen are an interracial couple who travel leading worship at churches and conferences.

They kept pressuring her until she broke down and told them the truth. Upon hearing her confession, they began to yell at her and threatened to break up the relationship. They gave her the choice that either she had to break it off or they would. If she refused, they vowed to disown her from the family and refuse to pay for her college education.

Her father, the cop, then started showing up at my job as intimidation, to demonstrate that he knew about me and he knew where I was. I never showed any fear, but this did leave me in a difficult position. I did not want my skin to be the cause of someone losing their family and being denied their dream in an education.

Not much later, she broke up with me. Three weeks after our breakup, she started dating someone else who, to her parent's satisfaction, was white. The following year they were married.

From then on, I decided to stand and fight to prevent anyone from going through anything like this. Since then I have been an advocate for racial reconciliation, not only in the community, but also in the Body of Christ.

I am now married to the love of my life who now joins me in that fight.

DAY 9

Purify My Heart

Heavenly Father, I come to you, knowing that it is your will that we all may be one, regardless of race, culture, or nationality. Jesus prayed that we all may be one, just as you and he are one, and that we may all be one in you. Father, I also know it is your will that your Body, the Church, be in unity. Your Word says how wonderful and pleasant it is when brothers and sisters live together in harmony!

Father, could it be that we are not one because of the issues of our hearts?

The Prophet Jeremiah wrote that the heart is deceitful above all things, and desperately wicked; who can know it? And your Word reminds me to guard my heart above all else, for it determines the course of my life. But, Father, you know my heart, and I'm asking you to please examine it and show me if there's anything that I may be carrying from the pain of injustice from my ancestors, or in my life that has caused a root of bitterness to grow. If so, I come to you in repentance so I can be free to love all of my brothers and sisters, regardless of race.

Father, I repent of all hatred and bitterness that I may have allowed to grow in my heart and caused me to not love your people as I should. I choose, now, to forgive all who have sinned against me, just as you have forgiven me. I ask, like King David, that you would create in me a clean heart, and renew a steadfast spirit within me, so that my heart will be pure and clean. I want a heart like yours, so I can love everyone, even my enemies, because I know in the end, love always wins.

Thank you, Father, for purifying my heart so that it may be filled with love, to love all people and help bring an end to racial divide in our nation. In Jesus' name, Amen.

(John 17:21; Ps. 133; Jer. 17:9; Prov. 4:23; Matt. 6:14; Ps. 51:10)

Gwen Campbell is the state prayer coordinator of North Carolina for Aglow International Ministries.

WHAT IS THE HOLY SPIRIT SAYING TO ME?

Love That Drives Out Hate

Father in Heaven, I pray Paul's words over the Church, "May the God of endurance and encouragement grant you to live in such harmony with one another, in accord with Christ Jesus, that together you may with one voice glorify the God and Father of our Lord Jesus Christ. Therefore welcome one another as Christ has welcomed you, for the glory of God" (ESV).

Father, my heart can hardly withstand the grace I have received through Christ. My judge has become my Father. I was once your enemy, unable to obey or please you, but now I'm your child, and Jesus—the King of heaven and earth—is my brother! Jesus welcomed me. Jesus shares everything with me. The dust of death rested on everything I touched, but now I'm an heir to divine glory. I once lived to satisfy animal cravings, driven by fear and suspicion, but now my mind is set on the Spirit, controlled by him who is peace and life. And I have been given a new family! I belong to countless others from every ethnic group and language, and we are compelled to rejoice in these mercies! We are one Church! And with all the saints and angels, we eagerly await your return.

But today I groan. The earth is in turmoil. Our cities burn. Rage fills the streets. A plague harasses us. Self-doubt, self-loathing, violence, and the erosion of truth are unraveling our nation. My brothers and sisters of color are grieved and abused. You "looked for justice, but behold, bloodshed; for righteousness, but behold, an outcry!" (ESV). So, your love compels me to join the groans of creation, the groaning of your Spirit and the groaning of my brothers and sisters. I weep with those who weep. Longingly, patiently, we look forward to the day when you will

Bob Bakke is the lead pastor of Hillside Church in Bloomington, MN.

break the curse over the universe, free it from its bondage to death and violence and injustice and set all things right.

Until then, as an heir of Christ, I join my spiritual family to defeat hatred and pride, clothing myself with the love, humility and self-sacrifice of Jesus. I cry out with them for help. Our battle is not against flesh and blood. Hatred tears the world apart, but you died and rose again to defeat it. I rest in the certainty that your Spirit groans for me, praying for my weaknesses and that I fulfill your plans. The love of Christ compels me. "We know that we have passed out of death into life, because we love the brothers. Whoever does not love abides in death" (ESV).

Keep me focused on the integrity of my own life. See if there is any wicked way in me. Let me be quick to forgive and ask for forgiveness. Make me swift to defend the oppressed, and swifter still to be reconciled to my brothers and sisters—allowing nothing to stand between us. May my brothers and sisters never stand alone because of my cowardliness. I live and die to you, O Lord. But, remind me that I belong to my brothers and sisters, too. Because of them, also, I neither live nor die to myself alone.

(Rom. 15:5-7; Isa. 5:7; Rom. 8; Rom. 12:15; 1 John 3:14; Ps. 139:24)

WHAT IS THE
HOLY SPIRIT
SAYING TO ME?

Your Mercy Fills Us with Hope

Lord God Almighty, King of the Nations, of the Universe and All Eternity, there is no one like you! We humble ourselves, bowing before your sovereign majesty, realizing that in your awesome greatness you alone are the source of hope for nations in distress as ours is right now.

You told Israel that her wound was incurable and her injury beyond healing, yet in spite of her hopeless condition you promised to restore the nation to health and healing. You also said that if your people would humble themselves, pray, seek your face and turn from their wicked ways, you will hear, forgive and heal their land. You have brought healing and deliverance to nations in distress, torn by division and outright war, over and over throughout human history as intercessors have stood in the gap to pray out prayers you put in their hearts and mouths. In this way, amazingly peace and reconciliation have come about, even suddenly, when there was no hope.

We are trusting you now, agreeing with other brothers and sisters in Christ of all ethnic backgrounds, according to your promise, that America will be delivered from this awful atmosphere of hateful division that is tearing our country apart. We cry out to you for your mercy and protection over our government and society. Help us to see we are all Americans, not Republicans or Democrats or Independents, but one nation under God regardless of our skin color or sub-culture.

We agree in prayer that the arch-divider of humanity, the devil (*diabolos* "the one who divides") be bound and driven out of our nation to the feet of Jesus Christ who conquered him once and for all, shedding his blood for both our individual and corporate sins, so we can be free of the evil one's influence.

We affirm the victory of the Cross and take authority over this spirit of division that is behind the pitting of one social class or ethnic group against another; that inspires ideologies aiming to take down our government and abolish our cherished values in return for mob rule, chaos and destruction. We say "no" to that in the name of Jesus!

John Robb serves as chairman of the International Prayer Council and International Prayer Connect, a "network of networks" of prayer ministries and initiatives around the world that came into being just after 9/11. The IPC has arranged national, regional and global prayer efforts, connecting praying people from all ethnic groups and denominations.

Thank you, Lord Jesus, for sharing your authority with us. We use it now to call forth the redemptive purposes you have for America as we struggle with the current racial conflict. We turn our eyes upon you and believe you for good things to come that are beyond all we can ask or even imagine for your glory and the well-being of our nation! We thank and praise you for hearing us. Amen.

(Jer. 30:12, 17; 2 Chron. 7:13-14; Ez. 22:30;
Jer. 1:9-10; Matt. 18:18-19; Lk. 10:17-19; Eph. 3:20)

WHAT IS THE HOLY SPIRIT SAYING TO ME?

False Assumptions?

I remember an incident during my freshman year of high school that stood out to me. I was at a student government meeting where we were planning our school's annual Multicultural Festival. The meeting was with our advisor, in her cooking classroom, right after our last class.

She began explaining how, that year, she envisioned expanding the festival to showcase more than just different ethnic cultures and celebrate religious diversity, as well. "You know, like Christianity . . .," she remarked, holding her hand over to my friend Quincy, an African American, who, like myself, just so happened to be a Christian.

"And . . .," she scanned the room once more, her eyes moving past the white girl, and then past the black girl and finally landing on me: a scrawny Filipino boy still wearing his oversized school uniform shirt and wrinkled khakis just like everyone else. "And . . .," she reached out her hand toward me, palm facing up, her eyes widening as if she'd found brown gold and her brows settling in relief for having accomplished this mission of inclusivity, acknowledging before me and everyone else, " . . . Buddhism."

In that moment, I didn't know whether or not to laugh, as I've always done to cope with awkward situations, because this time I couldn't tell whether it was funny or not. I also wasn't sure whether or not to clarify that I wasn't a Buddhist, because it seemed like an honest misunderstanding. And I didn't know if it was even important enough to interrupt her announcement, anyway. So I just sat there, listening silently to everything else she had to say, just as I had always done before, nodding as if nothing went wrong and smiling as if unperturbed in the least.

Josiah Jordan is a 2018 graduate from Brown University with a B.A. in Philosophy and is expected to receive his M.Div. from Yale Divinity School in 2021.

"This year, we want to embrace the diversity of diversity and make sure that *you are represented as you*."

Instances like these continued to transpire even throughout my time at divinity school, a decade later.

On one occasion, I was on my way to find a seat at the back of the lecture hall for my Old Testament class. A student approached me and said, "Great job last Friday, preacher!"

I was confused because I hadn't met with him before, nor had I preached in any capacity the entire semester. I smiled warmly to acknowledge him and continued to find my seat.

"That was you who preached at chapel, right?" he prodded, noticing my lack of reciprocity.

I responded, "I don't think so."

I finally sat down as the professor finished writing a series of Hebrew words on the whiteboard, and I opened my email to see what had gone on in chapel last week.

And what I saw didn't just bother me—it made sense, because by that point, a decade later, I'd already gotten used to things like this and just had to learn to accept it.

"*Friday, January 24: LUNAR NEW YEAR – sermon by graduating student Nate Lee.*"

The thing about these stories is that my high school advisor and divinity school classmate were not white, as you might have thought. Both were black. It showed, at least to me, that false assumptions based on race are not necessarily a one-way street. Confusion, unsettling feelings, and even trauma from these encounters can be experienced by anyone.

WHAT IS THE **HOLY SPIRIT** SAYING TO ME?

▼

God search us.
Reveal to us the ways
we have been
complicit with racism.
Reveal to us the places
where values, prayers,
and actions don't align.

▲

We Lament

D ear Lord, help us to get it right this time. May we be a people of deep, fervent prayer. But also, make us a people of action. Let us not only pray, but endow us with courage to pray with our proverbial feet. Help us to trample on the sin of othering, to displace the sin of oppression, and to dispel the sin of racism out of us, the Church, and America.

John told us that If we confess our sins, you are faithful and just and you will forgive us our sins and purify us from all unrighteousness. So God, we confess.

God, we the Church have been complicit for long enough. For centuries slavery, oppression, and legislated racism have been possible in America. All of which the Church, has sometimes been complicit in fostering, preserving, and furthering. Because of our years of silence, apathy, and complicity tragedies like Ahmaud Arbery, Breonna Taylor, George Floyd, and Rayshard Brooks are possible. God help to break our allegiance with individual race and systemic racism.

Help us to understand the truth of your Word that tells us that if one member suffers, we all suffer together.

We lament these evils from our nation's past.

We lament mothers losing sons and daughters. For every holiday, family gathering and birthday that will never be the same, we lament.

We lament the fact the Church has been silent on this issue, when we should have led the cry against it. Complicit in things we should have named as sin, we lament.

We praise you Lord, that you are gracious and compassionate. You will not turn your face from us if we return to you! So we turn.

Josh Clemons is the co-executive director of One Race.

Father, forgive us for being people of conviction, without courageous follow through. Forgive us for obsessing over orthodoxy and neglecting orthopraxy. Forgive us for not living out the values of the kingdom. Forgive us for not living out a kingdom ethic in the public square.

God, search us. Reveal to us the ways we have been complicit with racism. Reveal to us the places where values, prayers, and actions don't align.

God, help us to live out the ethic of the gospel. To love one another well. God help us, to mend a broken past. To go forth and make wrong things right. God help us to play our part in ending systemic oppression. God help us to be concerned with ethnic communities beyond what is happening on the news. God help us to live righteously and to do justly before you! It's in Christ name I pray, Amen.

(1 John 1:9; 1 Cor. 12:26; 2 Chron. 30:9; Micah 6:8)

WHAT IS THE
HOLY SPIRIT
SAYING TO ME?

DAY 13

Wake Us Up

Father, in Ephesians 5:14 you command and promise us: "Wake up, sleeper, rise from the dead, and Christ will shine on you." Even so, in the face of the rising revolution in race relations across our nation right now, we pray:

Show your people, especially black and white, how to WAKE UP to CHRIST *enough* to open wide our hearts and our churches to him in new ways, so that together we restore him to his rightful place among us in the life of the Church and prepare the way for his essential, irreplaceable role in healing and reconstituting race relations in our land.

Summon your people in this nation, especially black and white, to WAKE UP to CHRIST *enough* to gather in his presence and before his throne to listen to and understand one another better; to openly share our pain and brokenness with one another as well as our hopes and dreams; to unconditionally confess our sins against one another; to invite the Holy Spirit to bring about repentance, cleansing, reconciliation, new beginnings and long-term redemptive solutions for the racial challenges we face in the Church and in our nation.

Cause your people in this nation, especially black and white, to WAKE UP to CHRIST *enough* to become proactively involved for his sake in advancing his kingdom by publicly standing side by side in his name to confront and address, to reverse and restore the extensive, pervasive damages of our nation's "original sin"—slavery.

Allow your people in this nation, especially black and white, to WAKE UP to CHRIST *enough* to become sorely sorrowful, realizing that one race brutally oppressing another is fundamentally a sin

David Bryant is president of Proclaim Hope!, the founder of ChristNow.com, and the author of *Christ Is NOW.*

against *the living Christ himself*. Help us to be broken over how centuries of the plague of racism *inside* the Church has dishonored, distorted, and disgraced the Lord of Glory before the eyes of the nation.

Call your people in this nation, especially black and white, to WAKE UP to CHRIST *enough* to enter together into fresh, dynamic manifestations of his active reign breaking through here and now; to see as the gospel spreads in more powerful, society-transforming ways causing Americans of all colors to reach out anew; to receive in their own lives the saving power of the Lamb seated on the throne of heaven.

Answer all these appeals by bringing forth a nation-wide Christ Awakening movement in keeping with the vision of Colossians 3:11. May it connect black and white Christians in a vital synergy in which black lives really DO matter (and in turn all lives matter) BECAUSE, first of all, *Christ's life matters*—because his risen, reigning life infuses everyone who belongs to him. Therefore, with great hope we proclaim:

In this new creation of God's design there is no distinction between Greek and Hebrew, Jew or Gentile, foreigner or savage, slave or free man. **Christ is all that matters for Christ lives in them all. AMEN.**

Perfect Us in Unity

Father, we confess we have not carried your heart for unity as Jesus expressed it in John 17. We've made it a side issue, a nice thought, and not the great burden of Jesus' heart and life immediately before he faced the Cross.

During this season of uncertainty, we cry out to you to take us to the same depth of loving unity with one another as Jesus shared with you, Father. He prayed for nothing less than a *perfection* in unity that would stun the world with the love of God as seen in the radiant lives of his people. Give us the color blindness of the God-head toward every race and ethnicity we encounter—to learn from their strengths and help with their heart-felt needs.

Lord, our world desperately needs to know the truth about you. They need to understand there is a Savior—Jesus Christ—who will wipe away their guilt and shame and free them through the power of love and forgiveness.

Help us, dear Father, to be life-giving messengers of reconciliation who believe that those who unite others in the love and blessing of God will make the greatest contribution to world history by fulfilling the longest prayer of the Savior.

Lord Jesus, please help us answer your prayer by supernaturally making us one.

(John 17:21-23; 17:1-5; Eph. 2:1-10; 2 Cor. 5:20; John 17:23)

Dr. Ron Boehme is an ordained minister who has served with Youth With A Mission (YWAM) since 1974. He has founded works in the nation's capital, and the states of Virginia and Washington.

WHAT IS THE **HOLY SPIRIT** SAYING TO ME?

A Quiet Walk
Marred by Racism

As we all know, in March 2020, the Governor of California issued a mandatory stay-at-home order, due to the COVID-19 pandemic. Because of this, racism against Asian-Americans was already pretty high. People of Asian descent were being blamed for bringing the coronavirus to America, and other parts of the world.

On the evening of April 7, 2020, I took a walk with my wife, Juno, our 12-year-old son, Drew, and 5-year-old daughter, Nia, in our La Crescenta, California neighborhood. As we made our way down a quiet residential street, I noticed a tall white man walking up toward us. I immediately noticed that he was giving us "hard looks" from afar.

As we got near and proceeded to pass him, he looked at us and asked what we were looking at.

I calmly let him know that we weren't looking at anything, especially not him. He then started spitting out his hate toward us. "[Bleep] you Asians with your Coronavirus! Go back to China, or wherever the hell you came from!"

"What did you say?" I angrily shot back.

He looked at me and snarled, "You heard me. You're the reason we're in this mess to begin with!"

When my wife heard him say this, she was a bit shocked. She knew about the racist attacks happening to Asians around the world, due to COVID-19, but she never thought that it would happen in her quiet little town. I've been telling her for years that there were racists living here among us, even prior to COVID-19. I remember her brushing me off, telling me that it was "all in my head." Now she had a front seat to a racist act, directed toward her and her family.

I told the guy to leave. He then became really upset. I guess he couldn't accept the fact that an Asian man told him to leave. He told me to "shut up and go eat some rice."

He said all this while my two children were watching. They were very afraid. They never experienced anything like that in their entire young lives.

I started to feel my blood boil. I told him to shut up and to just leave. He then started approaching me in a very threatening manner, while telling me he was going to "[bleep] me up." It was around this time when my wife grabbed her phone and started recording.

As he approached, I put my hands up and squared off. I don't consider myself a fighter, but I was prepared to hit him with everything I had if he laid a finger on me or my family.

Residents started coming outside of their homes to witness the event unfolding. They, too, were beyond shocked that this was happening in their own neighborhood.

Once I showed him I was willing to fight back, I think it took him a little by surprise. He clearly wasn't expecting me to fight back. He thought I was going to just walk away with my tail between my legs. There was no way that I was going to be a victim that day.

He started to back away, all the while saying things to infuriate me even more. I also continued to taunt him as well, because I wanted him to hit me. I won't lie to you, I dared him to swing, because if he did, I would have legally been able to defend myself. But the swing never came. He definitely thought twice about it.

I came to the realization that he was nothing more than a schoolyard bully. He barked a good bark, but when it was time to bite, he didn't deliver. Once he got it through his head that I wasn't backing down, he started walking away, all the while continuing to mutter his racist rants. He was a big coward preying on the weak. I refused to show any signs of weakness because I would not be victimized.

Sam Han is from Los Angeles, CA and works as a freelance assistant editor for reality television. In his free time, he enjoys watching movies and spending quality time with his family.

Looking back on it now, I wish I handled the situation better, especially in front of my kids. The smart thing to do was to walk away and leave it alone. But at the same time, I didn't want to teach my kids that this sort of behavior was acceptable. I wanted to teach them to stand up for themselves when things like this happen.

WHAT IS THE
HOLY SPIRIT
SAYING TO ME?

▼

Compel me to listen

and learn with love;

to be quick to listen

and slow to speak.

Help me to hear their heart,

to remove any sinful robe

of judgment or offense

that is not mine to wear.

▲

Show Me the Way to Walk

eavenly Father, we read in Jeremiah 22:3 to "Do justice and righteousness, and deliver the one who has been robbed from the power of his oppressor. Also do not mistreat or do violence to the stranger, the orphan, or the widow; and do not shed innocent blood in this place" (NASB).

Lord, in this verse and throughout Scripture, you command us to do what is right and righteous, to bring what you have designed and declared in heaven into the realities of everyday life for every person on earth. Please search me, show me, and forgive me where I have been an obstacle instead of an instrument of your will. Holy Spirit, prompt me to pray as soon as I see a lack of your love, will, and ways.

As I lift my prayer and incline my ear to you, please teach me how to speak up and step up so that your will and your glory fills the earth. Pour out your wisdom so I would know and speak your truth. Please give me knowledge that brings the necessary humility and courage to step into conversations and situations where I may not be welcomed. Compel me to listen and learn with love; to be quick to listen and slow to speak. Help me to hear their heart, to remove any sinful robe of judgment or offense that is not mine to wear. I tear it before you and repent of attitudes that are not filled with the fruit of your Spirit.

Jesus please give me understanding to know how to work out and walk out the kind of love and truth that you modeled and mandated in your earthly ministry and even now as you are interceding for me at the right hand of the Father. You know all I need; you are all I need. Help me to remember that I lack nothing to do your will

Kathy Branzell is the president of the National Day of Prayer Task Force.

with your Spirit dwelling in me and empowering my every thought and action with the same power that brought you out of the grave. Give me meekness that walks in your authority and under your authority so that all the world sees is you, as you use me each day to bring a voice of power, peace, kindness, and relationship to the victims of oppression, violence, abandonment, loss, and lack. Help me to steward the resources and gifts you have given to me to be multiplied to all who bear your image, value, and purpose. In Jesus Name and for His glory I pray. Amen!

(Jer. 2:23; Lk. 11:2; Eph. 1:19; John 3:30)

WHAT IS THE
HOLY SPIRIT
SAYING TO ME?

Unity of the Body

Father, the world we live in has been twisted out of joint. Your Body has often fallen to the same fate. Dislocated from one another we wander aimlessly trying to be effective in ministry as the Body, but a body disjointed cannot function.

Help our witness. Jesus, you prayed to your Father "that [we] will all be one, just as you and I are one—as you are in me, Father, and I am in you. And may they be in us so that the world will believe you sent me" (NLT). The effect of the true unity of the Body of Christ is our witness to the world that you were sent. May we embrace the prayer of Jesus to become one.

May it not be solely in proximity, but may we be close in spirit. Just as the apostle Paul wrote, "There is one body and one Spirit, just as you were called to one hope when you were called; one Lord, one faith, one baptism; one God and Father of all, who is over all and through all and in all" (NIV). Our desire is to be a functioning body, that focuses on what we have in common rather than what our differences may be. May the evidence of our message be how we love one another, how we serve one another, how we accept one another. We desire to embrace unity for the sake of those who need to believe that you were sent to save them. I pray this in Jesus' name. Amen.

(John 17:21; Eph. 4:4-6)

Eli Bonilla is the national millennial director for the National Hispanic Christian Leadership Conference and the English pastor at Abundant Life Church of God in San Antonio, TX.

WHAT IS THE
HOLY SPIRIT
SAYING TO ME?

Tear Down the Dividing Wall

Our Father, your Holy Word says, *"But now in Christ Jesus, you who were far away have been brought near by the blood of Christ. For He is our peace, who made both groups one and tore down the dividing wall of hostility"* (HCSB). Our Lord Jesus Christ, we thank you for your blood that draws us into the presence of the Father. We also thank you that you are the Prince of Peace who was able to tear down the dividing wall between the Jews and the Gentiles.

Oh God, since you did this, we know that you can also bring your people together regardless of the color of our skin or the language we speak. So we ask you now for every person, no matter our skin color or ethnic group, to see that Jesus has already torn down the walls of hostility and separation between us through his death and resurrection.

Therefore, we ask you now, Lord Jesus Christ, to replace all prejudice with complete acceptance, replace any hostility with the peace of Christ, and replace any hate with the unconditional love of Jesus.

May we realize that God loves all people; therefore, we should also love all people, and by this love the world will know we are his disciples.

Our God and Father of our Lord Jesus Christ, we call upon you boldly,

Dr. Ronnie Floyd is the president and CEO of the Executive Committee of the Southern Baptist Convention.

asking you to bring us together! Make us one, even as you and Christ Jesus are one. Lead us to walk together in unity. Lead us to address the things that divide our community. Lead us to please you in every way. Lead us to follow your Word. God, may your favor be upon us as we strive to be more like Jesus. In Jesus' name. Amen.

(Eph. 2:13-14; Isa. 9:6; John 13:35)

WHAT IS THE
HOLY SPIRIT
SAYING TO ME?

We Receive
One Another

Now may the God who gives perseverance and encouragement grant you all to be of the same mindset toward one another according to Christ Jesus.

(Rom. 15:5, author's translation)

Faithful God of the ages, again and again you have strengthened the hearts of your people with your own steadfast courage. Now, in this bewildering time, our gatherings are disrupted, leaving us wondering if we are divided or united. Grant to us the same servant mindset of our Lord Jesus. Make us eager to honor. Make us swift to forgive. Train us to walk in his ways of open-hearted kindness. Only with the mind of our risen, living Lord is there hope that we will overcome differences to enjoy a unity of heart, voice, and purpose.

. . . so that with one united passion you may with one voice glorify the God and Father of our Lord Jesus Christ.

(Rom. 15:6, author's translation)

We know how to say nice and proper things about others. We are sincere as we repeat our scripted prayers. But at times you have enthused your people with a joyous, united yearning—that you would be known by all, and be loved by many. Oh, that you would align our desiring for your great Father-heart to be praised by every language and lineage, by every race, and in every place.

. . . receive one another, just as Christ also received us to the glory of God.   (Rom. 15:7, author's translation)

At the extravagant cost of Christ's blood, you have received us as forgiven sinners. Your love has lifted us to serve you as beloved worshipers. As you look upon us, we are more than merely equal. Before you, we are precious. Grant

Steve Hawthorne is the president of Waymakers, and the author of the *Seek God for the City* **annual prayer initiative.**

us that same kind of honoring grace to gladly receive people from different cultures and countries. Make us ready for relationship with the entire human family. Be pleased to make the fellowship of Christ-followers to become a spectacle of your love throughout our community and your world. In Jesus' name. Amen.

WHAT IS THE
HOLY SPIRIT
SAYING TO ME?

Names Can Hurt

A s a Korean American, I grew up in Dallas, Texas, during a time when diversity was expanding.

Despite being immersed in such diversity, growing up was not always easy. I remember as early as Kindergarten that my peers would ask me: "Are you Chinese; are you Japanese; are you Vietnamese? Never once did they ever ask if I was Korean. I never understood then why they wouldn't ask me about my ethnicity, but I just brushed it off as ignorance.

As I got into middle school and high school, the questions continued. Because of my last name, Lee, I would get asked, "Oh are you related to Jet Li?"

It was like I never could catch a break. It was then when name calling such as "Chink" or "Chino" was thrown at me all the time. Latinos made up most of my high school soccer team, and because I was the only Asian, I was soon given the nickname "Chino." Eventually it intensified when members of my team would often poke fun of me during practice saying, "Hey Chino, open your eyes!"

But I will never forget the many racial encounters I had while I was in college. One time while volunteering at the Texas Motor Speedway, a drunk, elderly white man called me back to the table for help by saying, "Hey Jackie Chan, come over here." But the one that caught me by surprise was when I was about to walk into a Jimmy Johns sandwich shop and an elder white said straight into my face, "Ching, Chong, Chang!"

Whether they were racist or just ignorant, ignorance cannot be corrected if the individual does not seek to be educated and corrected.

Alex Lee is the owner of God Knows Apparel, a street wear brand based in Dallas, TX which aims to make a change through clothing.

WHAT IS THE **HOLY SPIRIT** SAYING TO ME?

With Contrite Hearts,
We Cry Out

Heavenly Father, our human minds can hardly fathom that you, the Almighty and Eternal God, have invited us to approach your throne of grace with confidence 24/7, 365 days a year! We acknowledge that there is no God like you. Not one! When we consider that you have given us—as Your children— eternal life and the mind of Christ, our desire this moment is for our heart of prayer to match yours. We want the end result of our prayer time together to be for your kingdom to come and your will to be done, on earth as it is in heaven.

O, Lord, as we awaken each morning and go about our ways, we see and hear more and more about the path our nation appears to be heading on . . . and our hearts are breaking. Yet, honestly, we often feel helpless to make any real difference because of our own struggles with personal prejudices and selfish attitudes toward other people who are not just like us. Forgive us, Father, as your children, when we choose to allow worldly pleasures and pursuits to dominate our thoughts and actions toward others. Jesus, that was not your chosen path, because of your love for others. And we do desire to follow in your steps.

Forgive us, Lord, when we regularly make our prayers all about ourselves, and fail to be concerned enough to pray for our neighbors and those in various positions of authority! Lord, your Word speaks clearly that we are all easily deceived. Our nation and neighbors are desperate for your spiritual healing. Forgive us of the actions and attitudes toward others that come out in our personal life choices that grieve you.

We cry out for your forgiveness and healing in America from "each doing what is right in his own eyes," regarding color, class, and culture. May our nation repent of not seeking your kingdom and righteousness first and foremost. Too often, we choose our own wisdom, instead of yours, in everyday living. This results in division and disunity, hatred and murder, oppression and racism, confusion and chaos.

With contrite hearts, we repent of all these sins and return to you, O, Lord. Because you tell us to cry out to you, and we will be forgiven, please hear our cry. Thank you, Lord, that when we repent and do return to you, your Word promises that our sins may be wiped away, in order that times of refreshing may come from your presence, O Lord. In Jesus' name I pray. Amen.

Dennis and Betty Jo Conner are the co-founders of Called to Serve, a ministry that assists churches in becoming houses of prayer.

(Ps. 90:2; 2 Sam. 7:22; Heb. 4:16; Rom. 8:15; John 3:16; 1 Cor. 2:16; Matt. 6:10; Ps. 5:3; Prov. 14:12; Rom. 7:14-25; Col. 2:6-8; Rom. 8:38-39; 1 John 4:19; 1 Pet. 2:21; 1 Thess. 5:17; 1 Tim. 2:1-2; Prov. 16:25; Jdg. 21:25; Jas. 2:1-4; Matt. 6:33; Jas. 3:13-17; Ps. 51:17; Acts 3:19)

WHAT IS THE
HOLY SPIRIT
SAYING TO ME?

Heal and Reconcile

F ather, your Word says that after we have suffered a little while, the God of all grace, who has called us to his eternal glory in Christ, will himself restore, confirm, strengthen, and establish us. We come to you, Father, in our time of need to say thank you for calling us into your eternal glory. We thank you for your promise to restore, confirm, strengthen, and establish us as your people. We stand in agreement with the declaration of scripture, affirming your Lordship and dominion.

As we look at our world that is filled with pain and suffering, we remember your faithfulness to all generations. While our streets are filled with rage and riots, we remember your righteousness.

Father, we cry out for your healing power to fill our nation and to heal the heart of your Bride. We repent for our grumbling and complaining and for allowing eternity in so many moments to be nothing more than an afterthought.

Today, we refocus our hearts and our eyes on your splendor, your glory, your beauty and your dominion. We trust in your everlasting covenant promises of redemption even while it seems our world is drifting into deeper darkness.

We thank you that in every generation for the sake of your name, you reserve a remnant which will not bow its knees to Baal. In every era of history, you reaffirm your commitment to restoring your fellowship with mankind. We pray for an outpouring of the Holy Spirit in our individual lives that will lead us to love mercy, do justly and to walk humbly before our God.

We pray for un-offended hearts that will be given wholeheartedly to the cause of Christ, which is the ministry of reconciliation. Enable us by your power to do your will. Equip us for the work ahead. Let our hearts be anchored in the world to come. As you taught us to pray. Let your kingdom come, let your will be done in my nation, my city, my family and in my life as it is in heaven.

(1 Pet. 5:10-11; Micah 6:8, Matt. 6:9-10)

Brian Williams is a devoted husband and father. He also serves as the founder and senior pastor of Hope City House of Prayer and The Biblical Justice Institute.

WHAT IS THE HOLY SPIRIT SAYING TO ME?

Trading Prejudice for a Kingdom Legacy

There is none like you, God. As our gaze travels from your eyes of fire to your bronze feet, we are humbled and ashamed of our sin. We have treated our brothers and sisters as our enemies. We have allowed bitterness to take root and poison our thoughts, our deeds, our relationships. We have acted like the devil by stealing, killing, and destroying our brothers' and sisters' bodies, livelihood, property, income, self-worth—often even in your name, thereby calling evil as good.

We have made excuses for our behavior instead of taking ownership of our choices. We have succumbed to the schemes of the devil to divide us by the color of our skin, which is not how you see us. When you look at us, you see our heart, you hear our thoughts. We have shamed and dishonored the beauty of your creation.

Lord, this is not the legacy we want to leave. We desire to live a life free from all prejudice. To live a life that represents your throne—righteousness and justice being our foundation and love and faithfulness characterizing our person. We desire to dwell in unity and to be one with you. Help us, Lord. In the name of Jesus. Amen.

(Rev. 1:14-15; 1 John 4:20; Heb. 12:15; John 10:10; Isa. 5:20; Prov. 28:13; 1 Sam. 16:7; Ps. 139:1-2; Gen. 1:27; Ps. 89:14; Ps. 133:1; John 17:21)

Natasha Miller is the director of the Haggai Project and the author of *Praying What Jesus Says.*

WHAT IS THE
HOLY SPIRIT
SAYING TO ME?

The Subtlety
of Racism

W as I just called the "N" word in broad daylight while walking downtown in the Indiana city where I was attending law school? This majority "A" high school student—who won a University of Michigan Regents Alumni Award, now University of Michigan graduate, who believed in Jesus Christ and came from a loving home who taught me to behave like a lady, and to obey parents, elders, and the law—was in shock.

I was called the "N" word for doing nothing but being a female walking alone in the downtown area in the town where I was starting law school. It was 1977, and this was the first time I was called the "N" word to my face.

I knew that many of my fellow students assumed we blacks were there at law school as a result of "affirmative action" and they believed that I and others probably had taken the seat of some more deserving white student. Still, I was shocked and angry. I wanted to confront my accuser, but I was alone. They were with a group and just walked by. So I quickly walked away.

Years later, in early 2000, having practiced law for a few years I decided to pursue my interest in writing and attended a major Christian writers' conference in Eastern Pennsylvania. The conference was great. One afternoon I sat with a group of white writers and presenters. I don't recall how we began talking about the state of racial affairs, but I have never forgotten their comments. The attitude was that since I was a Christian and young black woman attorney I would agree to the false belief that discrimination and racism was somehow no longer a real problem. The black race "had overcome." Well I begged to differ. Nothing was further from the truth.

Linda Fegins is an attorney, an author, a prayer leader and intercessor on the Global Prayer Missions Force.

My female colleagues and I believe that there are numerous subtle, yet insidious, examples that we experience from white colleagues, even in our beloved legal system. Most arose not because we were women, but because we were *black* women. We were intentionally taught from home and learned that we had to work twice as hard and be twice as good as our white colleagues to get the fair recognition we had earned or deserved.

One such subtle act of discrimination happened to my colleague who was attending a deposition on a high-level complex case. When she arrived in the room, there were five white male attorneys, three white women, and her. An attorney of the host law firm appeared in the conference room where all awaited. He gave a brief review and then he walked over to my friend and asked "Are you my court reporter?"

"No," she responded. "I am one of the attorneys on this case."

This is a common experience.

Interestingly, the following week, my colleague was at the courthouse in Detroit and the same attorney who questioned her rode in the elevator with her. He spoke up and asked her if she remembered him. She replied that she did. To her surprise, he apologized, and said "What I said was racist and sexist; but more so racist." She was shocked.

WHAT IS THE
HOLY SPIRIT
SAYING TO ME?

_____

_____

_____

_____

_____

_____

_____

_____

_____

_____

_____

_____

_____

_____

_____

_____

_____

_____

_____

_____

_____

_____

_____

_____

_____

▼

We ask for an empowering

of the Holy Spirit throughout

the Body of Christ,

so that your Church will no longer be

conformed to and infected by

the status quo thinking of the world.

We desire to be truly and

radically transformed—

each of us, all of us, our congregations

and communities, our country—

by the renewing of our minds.

▲

Become Prophetic, Not Political

G lory to you, our Almighty God who created the human race "in your likeness." Praise to you Lord Jesus, our Blessed Hope, who broke the curse of evil and sin and will one day rule all in perfect righteousness.

Fill us, Holy Spirit, as we pray against the sin of racial superiority that continues to produce division, distrust, and distress in every sector of our culture and across our country. Convict us so that our words (and also our works) begin to more perfectly reflect the mind of Christ and the will of our Father in heaven. That we would not merely teach and preach "Love God; love your neighbor," but live it.

We ask you for forgiveness:

▶ for the sins of our founders, who immigrating from a foreign country, so callously conquered the inhabitants of a land we have thoughtlessly consumed.

▶ for the pain slaves were forced to endure for the sake of our economy and the comforts of their owners.

▶ for the advantage our culture gave (and often still does) to a select group of people while denying full access to freedom and justice to other citizens, based solely on the shade of their skin.

▶ for our sin of separation from one another and the heart-attitude of superiority, even hate, that divides not only our nation but has infiltrated and infects the Body of Christ.

We respond with contrition for our personal sin, whether by overt action or heartless apathy, but also with lament over our nation's disgrace.

Phil Miglioratti is the curator of the #ReimagneFORUM@Pray. Network and the founder of the National Pastors' Prayer Network.

We ask for an empowering of the Holy Spirit throughout the Body of Christ, so that your Church will no longer be conformed to and infected by the status quo thinking of the world. We desire to be truly and radically transformed—each of us, all of us, our congregations and communities, our country—by the renewing of our minds.

Change the way we think about *"We the people," "Liberty and justice for all,"* and *"Life, liberty and the pursuit of happiness."* We declare these are truly inalienable rights endowed by you *for every person and people group*. Reform us so that our praying, our living-working-playing, our Gospel message, and yes, even our political perspectives, demonstrate, oh God, that your will is good for all of us and perfectly suited to every human being.

With yielded hearts we ask that you lead us on a journey to:

▸ Reimagine what it means that all people are created in the image of God.

▸ Rethink how these truths should compel us to reshape your Church to be prophetic not political.

We ask in faith, with hope, knowing your love is covering a multitude of our sin. We give thanks for your grace and forgiveness. Now and always praying in the authority and name of Jesus our reconciler and unifier. Amen.

(Gen. 1:27; Matt. 22:36-40; Rom. 12:2)

WHAT IS THE HOLY SPIRIT SAYING TO ME?

▼

Forgive us for the way

we have ignored you,

and your heart for

justice and mercy,

especially toward the

poor and marginalized.

We repent of pride, selfishness,

hatred, and division,

and we turn to Jesus.

▲

Remove the Planks

Heavenly Father, thank you for making us in your image, and for giving every individual dignity and honor. From the beginning, you have called us to rule with you, yet we have selfishly chosen to rule over one another, giving way to violence and death. Forgive us for the way we have ignored you, and your heart for justice and mercy, especially toward the poor and marginalized. We repent of pride, selfishness, hatred, and division, and we turn to Jesus.

Jesus, thank you for the cross. Thank you for giving up the privilege of heaven to be called a friend of sinners. Thank you for reconciling us to God and each other through the cross. Thank you for calling us to the ministry of reconciliation. Empower us by the Holy Spirit to love, as you have loved us.

Holy Spirit, thank you for giving us life to live as those who were bought with a price. Forgive us for the times we have walked away from the mirror of Scripture, keeping the plank in our eye while judging the speck in our brother's. Forgive us for putting our needs above others. We pray for supernatural wisdom, power, and love. Enable us to be quick to listen, slow to speak, and slow to become angry; to practice true religion by loving the disadvantaged of our world. Help us to put feet to our faith by your power to see God's Kingdom come on earth as it is in heaven—and may we bring that reality to bear each day as we seek to love our neighbor as we love ourselves. In Jesus' name. Amen.

(Gen. 1:26-27; Ps. 8;
Gen. 1:28, 2:15, 3:16, 4:8-11;
Jer. 22:3; Prov. 31:8-9; Amos 5:7;
Phil. 2:5-7; Mk. 15:28; Col. 1:19-20;
Eph. 2:12-16; 2 Cor. 5:17-19;
Eph. 5:1-2; John 13:15; Rom. 8:12-17;
Jas. 1:22-25; Matt. 7:3-5; Phil 2:4;
Jas 1:5; 2 Tim. 1:7; Jas 1:19, 26-27;
Matt. 6:9-10; Lk. 10:27; Gal. 5:14)

Nick Hall is an evangelist, the president of Pulse and the chairman of The Table Coalition.

WHAT IS THE **HOLY SPIRIT** SAYING TO ME?

Revive Our Hearts with Righteousness and Justice

Father in heaven, we bow before you humbly, in the midst of our great need for your presence and healing in our nation. Our hearts are broken for our divided nation. We come before you in repentance on behalf of our hurting nation. Recognizing your holiness, we see our desperate need. *"Righteousness and justice are the foundation of your throne; love and faithfulness go before you" (NIV)*

We ask boldly for you to show forth your character and presence in us in these days of brokenness and division. May we be an answer to Jesus' prayer before he went to the cross to purchase us, his beloved Bride, as he prayed *"that all of them may be one, Father, just as you are in me and I am in you. May they also be in us so that the world may believe that you have sent me. I have given them the glory that you gave me, that they may be one as we are one" (NIV)*.

Jesus, we ask you to open our hearts to receive your love, humility, and compassion, so we can give to those hurting, even when we don't fully understand. May you take us to a deeper level of identifying with people different than ourselves, to be bridges to their souls longing for peace and restoration in you. We know that you even now are praying for us to fulfill your desires and will that all may know you and your gift of salvation. *You are able to save completely those who come to God through you, because you always live to intercede for them.*

Holy Spirit, we ask you to fill us and empower us to radically demonstrate your glorious power and presence to bring justice and righteousness back to our nation. May you intervene and bring a great revival and repentance that will result in a mighty end time awakening in our nation! Just as the prophet Joel called the children of God to rend their hearts and return to the Lord, He ended with the words given in answer to his cry, *"And afterward, I will pour out my Spirit on all people. Your sons and daughters will prophesy, your old men will dream dreams, your young men will see visions" (NIV).*

Nancy Wilson is an international speaker and author who has ministered in 77 countries as a Global Ambassador for Cru. She is passionate about raising up the next generation of radical servants for Jesus.

We love, honor and trust YOU . . . THE GREAT, MIGHTY, COMPASSIONATE GOD, who *"is not slow in keeping his promise, as some understand slowness. Instead he is patient with you, not wanting anyone to perish, but everyone to come to repentance" (NIV).* Be glorified in and through us we pray, in Jesus name and for his glory! Amen.

(Ps. 89:14; John 17:21-22; Heb. 7:25; Joel 2:28; Acts 2:17; 2 Pet. 3:9)

WHAT IS THE HOLY SPIRIT SAYING TO ME?

The Token Engineer

I was the first African American electrical engineer hired in the Printed Circuit Board (PCB) Division at a Department of Energy (DOE) company in the Midwest. Officially, I integrated this all white department in the mid-1980s.

When asked what I did, I answered like most employees in my area, "We make the non-nuclear components for bombs."

This day was like most days. Our afternoon break routine was to saunter to the vending machine on the mezzanine to purchase a candy bar or to buy a freshly brewed cup of coffee. I was in a small group that included me and two white men: scruffy-bearded, round beer-belly Peter from Iowa, and fast-talking, slender Mike from Nebraska.

As we turned the corner to ascend a short flight of steps to the vending machine, Peter, nonchalantly, said, to me, "Luke, you know you are the token." Unsure how to respond to this remark, I did not say a word. In Peter's mind, I was not hired based on my merit and credentials; rather, I was simply an affirmative action box that was checked.

The next day during our afternoon routine walk to the vending machine, Peter apologized.

Dr. Luke Brad Bobo is director of strategic partnerships at Made to Flourish (Overland Park, KS). Dr. Bobo is an author, speaker, and regularly teaches for Cru's Institute of Biblical Studies and Covenant Theological Seminary (St. Louis, MO).

WHAT IS THE
HOLY SPIRIT
SAYING TO ME?

Rally My Heart to Reconcile

F ather, before I ask you to move toward reconciliation in my life with others who may not look like me, I want to thank you for beginning the work of reconciliation in the life of your people. From the very beginning, your desire was for people of all nations to worship you as united people. I thank you that Jesus, right before he went to the cross to secure my salvation, prayed for unity between me and others who may not think like me, look like me, act like me, or vote like me. Through Jesus, you have made it possible for a new family to be created. You are a God that desires unity and for that, I want to say thank you!

Please give me the desire to fight for reconciliation. I can only do this when I remember the unity you purchased through your son Jesus. Give me the desire to be eager to maintain the unity that is possible in the Spirit. Allow me to see that I can only do this through supernatural humility, gentleness, patience, and bearing with one another in love. When I feel like I can't do it, enable me to see that I can, because Jesus first displayed it toward me.

Remind me that Jesus humbled himself to the point of death, which now allows me to die to myself for others. Remind me that Jesus was patient toward me and it leads to my repentance. For that reason, I can now be patient with others around me. Remind me that I can now be gentle toward others because Jesus was gentle toward me like the Good Shepherd that he is. Help me, Father, to extend grace to others in this long journey of reconciliation while praising Jesus, who extended grace to me in love and continues to do so when I fall short of the mark.

Derrick DeLain is lead pastor of Proclamation Church in Antioch, TN.

We need you to help us with this because apart from you, we can do nothing. We only have the ability to seek reconciliation because Jesus has already reconciled us to himself. Lord God, help me to do this in the power of your strength, not my own. In the name of Jesus, I pray. Amen.

(Gen. 17:5-8; John 17:21; Eph. 2:11-18;
Phil. 2:8; Eph. 4:1-7; John 15:5; 2 Cor. 5:18)

WHAT IS THE HOLY SPIRIT SAYING TO ME?

DAY

26

Love That Unifies and Restores

Heavenly Father, we cry out to you and repent for the sin of racism in our land. Create in us a clean heart; remove a wrong spirit from us. We pray, Lord, for clean hearts and clean hands. We come before you and ask your Holy Spirit to examine our hearts and lives and remove any wrong thinking, bias, or prejudice from our hearts.

Lord, you told your disciples that they were to be known by their love. Love is the greatest attribute; our ability to do great works will fade, but love endures forever. Father, we ask for a supernatural download of your love. We do not just want to talk about love, but we want to practice real love. Your Word proclaims how good and pleasant it is when we dwell in unity. Father, let your people be the ones who walk in unity with their sisters and brothers. Let healing take place where there has been wrongdoing, and let your Church lead the way in bringing hope and restoration to our nation.

Your word proclaims that your people will be called the re-

Lewis Hogan is the president of United Cry, a ministry that calls Christian leaders to unify across denominational, racial, and generational lines to take responsibility for the spiritual condition of America through unified repentance, revival prayer, and engaging culture and government for awakening.

builders of broken walls and the restorers of streets. Lord give your people the wisdom and the strategies from heaven to bring healing to our cities that are so broken by the injustice of racism. Amos cries out for justice to roll down like waters and righteousness like an ever-flowing stream. Father, we cry out for your justice and righteousness to flood our land. You are a good God, whose mercies are new every morning and we cry out for mercy on this land. Heal our land, Father, we pray. In the mighty name of Jesus, Amen.

(Ps. 51:10; Heb. 10:22; Ps. 24:4; John 13:35; 1 Cor. 13;
1 John 3:18; Ps. 133:1; Isa. 58:12; Amos 5:24; Lam. 3:23)

WHAT IS THE HOLY SPIRIT SAYING TO ME?

Freedom for All

L ord, Jesus, in Nazareth to proclaim your ministry, you quoted Isaiah "The Spirit of the Sovereign Lord is on me, because the Lord has anointed me to preach good news to the poor. He has sent me to bind up the brokenhearted, to proclaim freedom for the captives and release from darkness for the prisoners, to proclaim the year of the Lord's favor and the day of vengeance of our God, to comfort all who mourn, and provide for those who grieve in Zion—to bestow on them a crown of beauty instead of ashes, the oil of gladness instead of mourning, and a garment of praise instead of a spirit of despair. They will be called oaks of righteousness, a planting of the Lord for the display of his splendor" (NIV).

I know that all Scripture comes from you, but Lord, I have always felt that this is your special passage. You came to set captives free and to bring the reign of God into every aspect of human life. I know that the people listening that day couldn't hear your message. We still struggle to hear that astonishing good news that forever changes not just individual lives but cultural and national structures. It changes the way we treat one another. It can change the systemic racism that so binds our nation.

Lord, we receive the call to proclaim your life and message to our nation and a world that still desperately needs to hear of your favor. Your message is our message! Teach us today to bind up the broken-hearted and to proclaim freedom and release for captives. We proclaim your favor and fearfully announce that there is indeed a day of the Lord's vengeance coming.

Lord, we want to serve in your power and anointing with a message and lifestyle that is counter cultural. We choose in your power to bring comfort to those who mourn, a crown of beauty instead of ashes, and bring a garment of praise instead of despair. May all that we do display your splendor and righteousness in our nation and the world.

David Butts is the chairman of America's National Prayer Committee and the president of Harvest Prayer Ministries.

(Isaiah 61:1-3)

WHAT IS THE HOLY SPIRIT SAYING TO ME?

Emmanuel, Show Forth Your Great Mercy

Oh, Great God and Father, from whom the whole family in heaven and earth derives its name, we acknowledge you as the Sovereign over history. As the First and the Last, you preside in holiness over the epochs of time. Thank you!

We understand that you have appointed the seasons and pre-determined the boundaries of our dwelling. Indeed, you are the one who decided the very blood lines through which we would enter the earth. Thank you!

Omniscient One, you foreknew the various trials that our ancestors endured. You have revealed yourself to them and to us as EMMANUEL. Thank you for being with us right now! So that faith would be perfected within us, please let the trouble of our present trials, produce a reach in our hearts for you! Abba Father, may our reach produce transformation from the inside out!

As our dwelling place throughout the generations and our refuge in every storm, we run into you. A strength to all who wait upon you, our hearts fail but you are our portion. Oh Lord our strength and our shield, would you arm us with power from on high as we trust in your lovingkindness? Because your mercy never fails, we ask for you to turn back the battle and cause our hearts to trust in you again.

Forgive us for leaning on our own understanding and pursuing justice and reconciliation within our own strength. We are guilty of what the prophet Jeremiah exhorted in that we have said, "Peace, peace, when there is no peace!" Forgive us for accepting temporal victories, drinking from broken cisterns, and settling for a pagan peace. We cry out to you today, Father, forgive us. We confess our guilt before you today with unveiled faces, because of your Son Jesus! With you there is mercy.

Jonathan Tremaine Thomas is a pastor, producer, and missionary entrepreneur. As the founder of Civil Righteousness, Inc., he leads racial reconciliation and revival initiatives around the country while residing in Ferguson, Missouri with his wife and their young daughter.

Oh Lord, the accumulated iniquities, wicked thinking, transgressions, and wicked actions of many generations weigh upon us day and night. Our senses are overwhelmed with grief from the assaults and the accusations. Though devastatingly broken, give us living hope in your abundantly great mercies that you will not utterly consume nor forsake us!

We pray *"Kyrie Eleison!" Lord Have Mercy on Us, Christ Have Mercy."* We ask for supernatural healing from all radicalized trauma and related historic post-traumatic stress. You are faithful, true, and just in all of your ways! As you show forth your mercy, heal our troubled bones, and grant us your salvation. We commit to do justly, love mercy, and walk humbly with you, oh God!

(Eph. 3:15; Acts 17:26; Isa. 7:4; Jas. 1:4; Ps. 90:1; Isa. 40:31; Ps. 73:26, 18:32, 3:5-6; Jer. 6:14; Jer. 2:13; Ex. 22:27; Isa. 90:8; 1 Pet. 1:3; Deut. 4:31; Neh. 9:31; Rev. 19:11; Ps. 85:7; Ps. 6:2; Micah 6:8)

WHAT IS THE
HOLY SPIRIT
SAYING TO ME?

▼

Forgive us for leaning on
our own understanding and
pursuing justice and reconciliation
within our own strength....
Forgive us for accepting
temporal victories,
drinking from broken cisterns,
and settling for a pagan peace.

▲

A Routine Stop?

When I was younger, I was pulled over by police. I had no criminal record, no weapons, and wasn't rude. I'm just an overall nice guy.

The officer asked me to turn off my headlights, then said he was giving me a ticket for driving without headlights. He then asked me for my driver's license. When I handed it to him, he threw it on the ground. Then he yelled over to his partner, "Hey, we have a boy over here driving without a license."

He asked me to step out of the car and to give him my other identification cards. When he saw my military ID, he got nervous and then told me to get back in the car and go home.

I drove home scared, afraid, powerless.

If he had not seen my military ID what might have happened next?

Maybe he would've sat on my neck for nine minutes while bystanders white and black begged them for mercy . . .

Maybe, after a while, I would plead to the policeman and tell him "I can't breathe," and he would just respond to me, "Relax." Maybe my final words would be heard on the video screaming for my mother . . .

Maybe the news reports would come out later and say, "I heard he was driving around at night without headlights. He must've been some type of drug dealer" . . .

Would anyone be there for my wife and children? Or would people be too busy arguing on Facebook about the right or wrong way to protest . . .

It brings tears to my eyes to think that one day my children would grow up and ask their mother to tell them stories about the father they never knew.

And that my children would have to grow up hearing statements like:

"It's 2020, racism is not that bad."

"If people would comply, cops would not hurt them."

Michael Johnson is a young adult ministry leader and has been mentoring college students for more than 20 years. He currently resides in North Carolina with his wife and three children.

My message is this: When your black and brown friends tell you their experiences and you wonder why it seems like they are always playing the race card, maybe it's because the race card is being played on them every day and you just don't see it. Maybe you don't fully understand? And that's okay.

It's not your fault that you don't understand. But it is your fault if you don't listen. If you close your ears because it makes you uncomfortable.

My advice to everyone during these times: Always listen in order to hear and understand. Pray for our society. Be vigilant, and never . . . ever . . . be silent in the face of injustice!

WHAT IS THE
HOLY SPIRIT
SAYING TO ME?

_____

_____

_____

_____

_____

Raise Up
Righteous Voices

F ather in Heaven, I thank you that I can enter boldly into your throne of grace and I can ask confidently for your kingdom of love and mercy to flood America at this hour. I take this moment to join your son Jesus, our eternal intercessor who is praying for us even at this moment. I come into full agreement with what Heaven is praying over my nation. I pray, "Let your kingdom come, and let your will be done on earth as it is in heaven."

Father, throughout history you have raised up voices of righteousness and justice to inspire a generation to change the culture of society; voices that pierce the darkness and confront sin. We remember world-changers like William Wilberforce who helped abolish slavery in his lifetime. We remember Dr. Martin Luther King Jr. and his righteous leadership during the civil rights movement.

I pray, oh Lord, that your eyes would search throughout the earth to strengthen those whose hearts are fully committed to you. Lord, where are the Wilberforces? Where are the MLKs who lead in boldness and the fear of the Lord?

Father, I ask for courageous leaders to rise up in this hour. I pray for the fear of God to be greater than the fear of man. I pray for strength and courage to gird the people of God at this time. Give us a backbone to stand for what is right and true. I pray we would not sway to left and right based on what is popular but instead, stand for what is Godly. Let righteous men and women be used as piercing voices of sobriety, conviction, and wisdom to help navigate the Body of Christ during this season. I pray out of James 1:5, that Christian leaders will be filled with wisdom from Heaven. When our world is confused and does not have an answer for the problems that we face, let the Church take lead.

Jason Nettles is the founder of Asia Rising. He is a YWAM missionary based in Southern California.

I pray my generation would unashamedly stand against racial injustice and inequality. I pray that our children would be proud of how we stood against the sin of racism in America. I pray the legacy of our children would be this as a reality, "We hold these truths to be self-evident, that all men are created equal, that they are endowed, by their Creator, with certain unalienable rights." Father, I echo the resilient prayer of Martin Luther King. "No, no, we are not satisfied . . . and we will not be satisfied until justice rolls down like waters and righteousness like a mighty stream." In Jesus' name, I pray. Amen.

(Heb. 4:16, 7:25; Matt. 6:10; 2 Chron. 16:9; Jas. 1:5; Amos 5:24)

WHAT IS THE **HOLY SPIRIT** SAYING TO ME?

Committed to
Listen, Learn, and Heal

Heavenly Father, we watch painful images on television and read news reports of those who cry out for justice. Our lack of awareness is suddenly magnified as we listen to stories from people who struggle with rejection and discrimination in our society. We are awakened to racial tensions that have rocked our world.

But we confess, oh, Lord, that our first response can easily be one of defensiveness or misunderstanding. I pray, first of all, for an outpouring of humility in my life. I know that as a believer I am chosen and dearly loved of God, and so my heart's desire is to represent your heart well to others. Please clothe me with compassion, kindness, humility, gentleness, and patience.

As I clothe myself with these Christ-honoring attributes, I pray I will learn to listen well. Let me hear the stories, process the pain and grief, and be slow to comment except with graciousness and love. May my responses demonstrate that I value each person as one who is precious in the sight of God.

And then, Lord, I pray for clarity and truth. Give me discernment to recognize and understand the true issues. You promise in Psalm 25:9 that you guide the humble in what is right and will teach us your way. There are differing opinions about what racial healing looks like, along with different perspectives and strategies to get there. We pray for your plan above all the other voices. You promise to be the voice of clarity when we seek you. We pray for the discernment that you offer—that in whatever direction we go, we will hear a voice behind us saying, "This is the way; walk in it."

As we walk according to your plan for racial healing, we pray for a revival of love and forgiveness. We know there is no fear in love because perfect love drives out fear. May we love well and deescalate fear and suspicion. And may forgiveness be a resounding clarion call to our nation. Forgiveness brings the cycle of racial healing full circle when we are kind and compassionate to one another, forgiving each other, just as in Christ, you forgave us. I commit myself to walk humbly in your plan to heal the racial divide in our nation. In Jesus' name. Amen.

(Col. 3:12; Isa. 43:4; Ps. 25:9; Isa. 30:21; 1 John 4:18; Eph. 4:32)

Carol Madison is editor of *Prayer Connect* magazine and the director of prayer ministries at Hillside Church of Bloomington, MN (a suburb of Minneapolis). She is also the author of *Prayer That's Caught and Taught.*

WHAT IS THE
HOLY SPIRIT
SAYING TO ME?

Make Us One

Heavenly Father, you alone are the source of life and grace. It's only by the power of your grace that we can fulfill your Son's prayer that we would be one, as you and he are one. I ask you today to pour out grace that we your people would walk worthy of the calling with which we are called.

Help us to embrace meekness, lowliness, and gentleness. Help us to embrace longsuffering and patience. I ask that you would enable and convict us to bear long with one another in love. It is only by your ability that we are able to overcome the inclinations of our flesh and mind and allow the Holy Spirit to bear the fruit of love through us. I ask that you give us the diligence to keep the unity of the Spirit in the bond of peace.

You and you alone can make your people one. I ask that today that a shift and a change would take place in the hearts of many of your people, that conviction would arise upon our souls calling us to humility and love. Convict us to consider others more valuable than ourselves, that we would embrace the mind of Christ, making ourselves servants of all, just like Jesus.

Thank you, Father, for releasing your power and grace in our lives. We believe that you are fulfilling your desires for oneness in your

Billy Humphrey is an intercessor for revival, co-pastor of NewBridge Church, and director of the International House of Prayer Atlanta, which offers 24/7 live worship and prayer and takes the gospel from the neighborhoods to the nations.

body. We agree with your heart and your desire. We thank you for having your way in the Church. Thank you for making us the dream of your heart, a pure and spotless Bride from every tribe, tongue, people, and nation. In the matchless name of your precious Son, Jesus. Amen.

(Eph. 4:1-3; John 17:11; Phil. 2:1-11; Rev. 5:9)

WHAT IS THE **HOLY SPIRIT** SAYING TO ME?

_____

_____

_____

_____

_____

_____

_____

_____

_____

_____

_____

_____

_____

_____

_____

_____

_____

_____

_____

_____

WHAT NOW?

ACTION STEPS
TO BE A VOICE FOR
RACIAL HEALING

"Produce fruit in keeping with repentance." (Matt. 3:8, NIV)

Now that you have walked through the 31-day prayer journey toward racial healing, let's get practical. You may be wondering, *what now? How do I walk out this inward heart transformation in my daily life?*

The fruit of a repentant and renewed heart is a new walk and a new talk. Here are three simple ways you can continually produce the biblical fruit of racial healing in your life, in your relationships, and in your sphere of influence.

1. Through prayer, be diligent in washing your heart with truth.

"Search me, O God, and know my heart! Try me and know my thoughts! And see if there be any grievous way in me, and lead me in the way everlasting!" (Ps. 139:23-24, ESV)

This is ultimately a heart issue. We cannot expect national healing or societal transformation without first confronting our own personal biases and prejudices. *We have to get real and allow God to deeply clean our hearts.* **We must continue to ask Him to anoint our eyes to see and love his image in every human being.** We can use this book as a reference to keep our hearts in check.

ACTION STEPS

---

2. Build diverse relationships.

"A new commandment I give you: Love one another.
As I have loved you, so you must love one another." (John 13:34, NIV)

A gift we can give to each other is ourselves—our time, our conversation, our love. ***We must be intentional in building deep and authentic relationships with people that don't look like us or think like us.***

Get to know them and hear their stories. Focus on understanding rather than just being understood. Invite them into your life, into your home, and invest in being a part of their lives as well. Strive for relationships that look like the Kingdom of heaven— multi-ethnic and multicultural. It's not easy, but choose to step out of your comfort zone and build these friendships.

3. Be a prophetic voice within your circles of influence.

"Speak up for those who cannot speak for themselves,
for the rights of all who are destitute. Speak up and judge fairly;
defend the rights of the poor and needy." (Prov. 31:8-9, NIV)

The Church is the moral conscience of the nation. Throughout history God has given the Church authority to call nations to higher moral standards. We must use our positions, platforms and power to stand against racism and discrimination of all forms—isolated or systemic.

Be a voice for the voiceless and stand up for righteousness and gospel justice. Being a prophetic voice won't always be popular or easy. We must pledge our allegiance to Jesus over acceptance, popularity, political ideology, and comfort. We must be willing to become informed on issues that fuel systemic racism

ACTION STEPS

and use our voices to confront such practices in our home, church, marketplace, and all other establishments.

May God bless you and his Holy Spirit empower you to continue to pray, and to be a catalyst for racial healing in your family, neighborhood, church, community and our nation!

WHAT IS THE
HOLY SPIRIT
SAYING TO ME?

ABOUT THE COMPILERS

Niko Peele is the founder and director of Ignite Movement, a Christian nonprofit that helps establish and advance vibrant Gospel communities and united movements on college campuses and in cities. Niko resides in Raleigh, North Carolina, with his wife, Carole Ann. They travel nationally, as well as internationally, calling young people to merge their passion for Jesus with Christlike action to see catalytic change in the world. Niko also serves on the leadership team for Collegiate Day of Prayer and is a member of America's National Prayer Committee.

Jonathan Graf is the president of PrayerShop Publishing and of the Church Prayer Leaders Network. He has been in prayer ministry for more than 25 years, working primarily with prayer leaders and churches helping them to grow to be houses of prayer. He has been a popular speaker on the subject of prayer, ministering in churches and conferences. Jon is the author or compiler of five other books on prayer. He resides in Brazil, Indiana, with his wife, JoLyn, where he particularly enjoys spending time with his three grandchildren.

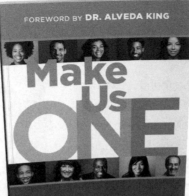

Pray *Make Us One* Together!

If you have been blessed by praying through *Make Us One*, why not purchase copies for your friends, your small group, or your congregation to pray together?

Be a force for transformation!

Multi-copy discounts are available at prayershop.org

PRAYERSHOP PUBLISHING

IGNITE
M O V E M E N T

TO SEE THE GOSPEL OF JESUS CHRIST
TRANSFORM COLLEGE CAMPUSES &
CITIES

JOIN THE MOVEMENT

LEARN HOW YOU CAN ADOPT A CAMPUS AT

WWW.IGNITEMVMT.COM